50 Small Steps, Big Flavors Recipes

By: Kelly Johnson

Table of Contents

- Garlic Butter Shrimp
- Mango Salsa Chicken Tacos
- Caprese Skewers
- Lemon Dill Salmon
- Spicy Sriracha Roasted Nuts
- Maple Glazed Brussels Sprouts
- Zesty Grilled Vegetables
- Honey Balsamic Glazed Chicken
- Avocado Toast with Poached Egg
- Crispy Parmesan Zucchini Fries
- Sweet Chili Chicken Wings
- Ginger Soy Grilled Pork Tenderloin
- Pesto Stuffed Mushrooms
- Greek Yogurt Chicken Salad
- Buffalo Cauliflower Bites
- Garlic Parmesan Roasted Potatoes
- Cilantro Lime Rice

- Crispy Chickpeas
- Tomato Basil Soup with Grilled Cheese
- Coconut Curry Shrimp
- Balsamic Roasted Tomatoes
- Lemon Garlic Hummus
- Sesame Crusted Tuna Bites
- Pineapple Teriyaki Chicken Skewers
- Crispy Fish Tacos with Lime Crema
- Spicy Roasted Sweet Potatoes
- Cheese Stuffed Peppers
- Avocado Mango Smoothie
- Roasted Red Pepper Soup
- Garlic Herb Butter Steak
- Cucumber Feta Salad
- Baked Avocado Eggs
- Miso Soup with Tofu
- Roasted Butternut Squash Soup
- Crispy Garlic Parmesan Brussel Sprouts
- Tomato Cucumber Salad with Feta

- Honey Mustard Chicken Bites
- Black Bean and Corn Salsa
- Spinach and Feta Stuffed Chicken
- Lemon Parmesan Asparagus
- Spicy Tuna Tartare
- Smoked Salmon Crostini
- Creamy Garlic Parmesan Mushrooms
- Roasted Carrot Hummus
- Bacon Wrapped Dates
- Buffalo Cauliflower Salad
- Apple Cinnamon Baked Oatmeal
- Pumpkin Spice Granola
- Crispy Fried Green Beans
- Lemon Basil Pesto Pasta

Garlic Butter Shrimp

Ingredients:

- 1 lb large shrimp (peeled and deveined)
- 2 tbsp butter
- 4 garlic cloves (minced)
- 1 tbsp olive oil
- Salt and pepper to taste
- 1 tsp red pepper flakes (optional)
- 2 tbsp fresh parsley (chopped)
- 1 tbsp lemon juice

Instructions:

1. Heat olive oil and butter in a large pan over medium-high heat.
2. Add minced garlic and cook for 1-2 minutes, until fragrant.
3. Add the shrimp to the pan in a single layer. Season with salt, pepper, and red pepper flakes.
4. Cook the shrimp for 2-3 minutes per side, until pink and opaque.
5. Remove from heat and stir in lemon juice and chopped parsley.
6. Serve immediately. Enjoy with rice or pasta!

Mango Salsa Chicken Tacos

Ingredients:

- 4 chicken breasts
- 1 tbsp olive oil
- 1 tsp chili powder
- 1 tsp cumin
- Salt and pepper to taste
- 1 cup mango (diced)
- 1/2 red onion (diced)
- 1 jalapeño (finely chopped)
- 1/4 cup fresh cilantro (chopped)
- 2 tbsp lime juice
- 8 small tortillas

Instructions:

1. Preheat the grill or a skillet to medium heat.
2. Rub the chicken breasts with olive oil and season with chili powder, cumin, salt, and pepper.
3. Cook the chicken for 6-7 minutes on each side, or until fully cooked (165°F internal temperature).
4. While the chicken cooks, prepare the mango salsa: in a bowl, mix together diced mango, red onion, jalapeño, cilantro, and lime juice. Season with salt to taste.

5. Once the chicken is done, slice it into strips.

6. Warm the tortillas in a pan or microwave.

7. Assemble the tacos by placing sliced chicken on each tortilla and topping with mango salsa.

8. Serve immediately and enjoy!

Caprese Skewers

Ingredients:

- 1 pint cherry tomatoes
- 8 oz fresh mozzarella balls (bocconcini or ciliegine)
- Fresh basil leaves
- Balsamic glaze (for drizzling)
- Olive oil (for drizzling)
- Salt and pepper to taste

Instructions:

1. Thread a cherry tomato, a mozzarella ball, and a fresh basil leaf onto small skewers or toothpicks.
2. Arrange the skewers on a platter.
3. Drizzle with olive oil and balsamic glaze.
4. Sprinkle with salt and pepper to taste.
5. Serve as an appetizer or a light snack. Enjoy!

Lemon Dill Salmon

Ingredients:

- 4 salmon fillets
- 2 tbsp olive oil
- 1 tbsp lemon zest
- 2 tbsp fresh lemon juice
- 1 tbsp fresh dill (chopped)
- Salt and pepper to taste
- Lemon wedges (for serving)

Instructions:

1. Preheat your oven to 400°F (200°C).
2. Place the salmon fillets on a baking sheet lined with parchment paper.
3. Drizzle with olive oil, lemon juice, and lemon zest. Sprinkle with fresh dill, salt, and pepper.
4. Bake for 12-15 minutes, or until the salmon flakes easily with a fork.
5. Serve with lemon wedges on the side.
6. Enjoy your bright, flavorful salmon!

Spicy Sriracha Roasted Nuts

Ingredients:

- 2 cups mixed nuts (almonds, cashews, pecans, etc.)
- 2 tbsp olive oil
- 2 tbsp Sriracha sauce
- 1 tbsp honey
- 1/2 tsp garlic powder
- 1/2 tsp smoked paprika
- Salt to taste

Instructions:

1. Preheat your oven to 350°F (175°C).
2. In a bowl, mix together olive oil, Sriracha sauce, honey, garlic powder, smoked paprika, and salt.
3. Add the mixed nuts to the bowl and toss to coat evenly.
4. Spread the nuts in a single layer on a baking sheet.
5. Roast for 10-15 minutes, stirring halfway through, until the nuts are golden and fragrant.
6. Let cool before serving. Enjoy!

Maple Glazed Brussels Sprouts

Ingredients:

- 1 lb Brussels sprouts (trimmed and halved)
- 2 tbsp olive oil
- Salt and pepper to taste
- 3 tbsp maple syrup
- 1 tbsp balsamic vinegar
- 1/4 tsp red pepper flakes (optional)

Instructions:

1. Preheat your oven to 400°F (200°C).
2. Toss the Brussels sprouts in olive oil, salt, and pepper.
3. Spread them on a baking sheet in a single layer and roast for 20-25 minutes, shaking the pan halfway through.
4. While the sprouts roast, whisk together maple syrup, balsamic vinegar, and red pepper flakes (if using).
5. Once the Brussels sprouts are roasted and crispy, drizzle the maple glaze over them.
6. Toss to coat and serve immediately. Enjoy!

Zesty Grilled Vegetables

Ingredients:

- 2 zucchinis (sliced)
- 1 bell pepper (cut into strips)
- 1 red onion (sliced into rings)
- 1 cup cherry tomatoes
- 2 tbsp olive oil
- 1 tbsp lemon juice
- 1 tsp dried oregano
- Salt and pepper to taste

Instructions:

1. Preheat the grill to medium-high heat.
2. In a large bowl, combine olive oil, lemon juice, oregano, salt, and pepper.
3. Add the vegetables to the bowl and toss until they are well-coated.
4. Grill the vegetables for 4-5 minutes per side, until tender and lightly charred.
5. Serve immediately, either on their own or as a side dish. Enjoy!

Honey Balsamic Glazed Chicken

Ingredients:

- 4 chicken breasts
- 2 tbsp olive oil
- Salt and pepper to taste
- 1/4 cup balsamic vinegar
- 2 tbsp honey
- 1 tsp Dijon mustard
- 1 garlic clove (minced)

Instructions:

1. Preheat your oven to 400°F (200°C).
2. Heat olive oil in a large skillet over medium-high heat.
3. Season the chicken breasts with salt and pepper, then cook them in the skillet for 4-5 minutes per side until golden.
4. While the chicken cooks, whisk together balsamic vinegar, honey, Dijon mustard, and minced garlic in a small saucepan.
5. Bring to a simmer and cook for 3-5 minutes until the glaze thickens.
6. Once the chicken is cooked, drizzle the balsamic glaze over it.
7. Serve with your favorite sides. Enjoy!

Avocado Toast with Poached Egg

Ingredients:

- 2 slices whole grain bread
- 1 ripe avocado (mashed)
- 2 eggs
- Salt and pepper to taste
- Red pepper flakes (optional)
- Fresh parsley (for garnish)

Instructions:

1. Toast the bread slices until golden and crispy.
2. While the bread is toasting, poach the eggs in simmering water for 3-4 minutes, until the whites are set but the yolk is still runny.
3. Spread the mashed avocado evenly on the toasted bread.
4. Top with a poached egg on each slice.
5. Season with salt, pepper, and red pepper flakes (if using).
6. Garnish with fresh parsley and serve immediately. Enjoy!

Crispy Parmesan Zucchini Fries

Ingredients:

- 2 zucchinis (cut into fries)
- 1/2 cup breadcrumbs (preferably panko)
- 1/2 cup grated Parmesan cheese
- 1 tsp garlic powder
- 1/2 tsp dried oregano
- 2 eggs (beaten)
- Salt and pepper to taste

Instructions:

1. Preheat your oven to 425°F (220°C).
2. In a bowl, mix together breadcrumbs, Parmesan, garlic powder, oregano, salt, and pepper.
3. Dip the zucchini fries into the beaten eggs, then coat with the breadcrumb mixture.
4. Arrange the coated fries in a single layer on a baking sheet.
5. Bake for 20-25 minutes, flipping halfway through, until crispy and golden.
6. Serve immediately with marinara sauce for dipping. Enjoy!

Sweet Chili Chicken Wings

Ingredients:

- 2 lbs chicken wings
- 2 tbsp olive oil
- Salt and pepper to taste
- 1/4 cup sweet chili sauce
- 1 tbsp soy sauce
- 1 tbsp rice vinegar
- 1 garlic clove (minced)
- 1 tsp grated ginger

Instructions:

1. Preheat your oven to 400°F (200°C).
2. Toss the chicken wings in olive oil, salt, and pepper, and arrange them on a baking sheet.
3. Bake for 25-30 minutes, flipping halfway through, until crispy.
4. While the wings cook, combine sweet chili sauce, soy sauce, rice vinegar, garlic, and ginger in a small saucepan. Bring to a simmer for 3-5 minutes.
5. Once the wings are cooked, toss them in the sweet chili sauce.
6. Serve immediately and enjoy!

Ginger Soy Grilled Pork Tenderloin

Ingredients:

- 1 lb pork tenderloin
- 2 tbsp soy sauce
- 1 tbsp honey
- 1 tbsp grated ginger
- 2 garlic cloves (minced)
- 2 tbsp olive oil
- 1 tbsp rice vinegar
- Salt and pepper to taste

Instructions:

1. In a bowl, whisk together soy sauce, honey, ginger, garlic, olive oil, rice vinegar, salt, and pepper.
2. Place the pork tenderloin in a resealable bag and pour the marinade over it. Let marinate for at least 30 minutes (or up to overnight in the fridge).
3. Preheat the grill to medium-high heat.
4. Grill the pork tenderloin for 12-15 minutes, turning occasionally, until it reaches an internal temperature of 145°F (63°C).
5. Let the pork rest for 5 minutes before slicing.
6. Serve with your favorite sides and enjoy!

Pesto Stuffed Mushrooms

Ingredients:

- 12 large mushrooms (stems removed)
- 1/4 cup pesto (store-bought or homemade)
- 1/4 cup cream cheese (softened)
- 1/4 cup grated Parmesan cheese
- 1/4 cup breadcrumbs (preferably panko)
- Salt and pepper to taste
- Fresh basil for garnish

Instructions:

1. Preheat your oven to 375°F (190°C).
2. In a bowl, mix together pesto, cream cheese, Parmesan cheese, breadcrumbs, salt, and pepper.
3. Stuff each mushroom cap with the pesto mixture.
4. Arrange the stuffed mushrooms on a baking sheet.
5. Bake for 20 minutes, or until the mushrooms are tender and the filling is golden.
6. Garnish with fresh basil and serve warm. Enjoy!

Greek Yogurt Chicken Salad

Ingredients:

- 2 cups cooked chicken breast (shredded or diced)
- 1/2 cup plain Greek yogurt
- 1/4 cup mayonnaise
- 1 tbsp Dijon mustard
- 1 celery stalk (diced)
- 1/4 cup red onion (diced)
- 1/4 cup dill pickle (chopped)
- 1 tsp dried dill
- Salt and pepper to taste
- Lemon juice (optional)

Instructions:

1. In a large bowl, combine the Greek yogurt, mayonnaise, Dijon mustard, and dried dill.
2. Add the cooked chicken, celery, red onion, and pickle. Stir to combine.
3. Season with salt, pepper, and a squeeze of lemon juice if desired.
4. Serve on bread, in wraps, or as a salad topping. Enjoy!

Buffalo Cauliflower Bites

Ingredients:

- 1 medium cauliflower (cut into florets)
- 1/2 cup flour
- 1/2 cup water
- 1 tsp garlic powder
- 1 tsp onion powder
- 1/2 tsp paprika
- Salt and pepper to taste
- 1 cup buffalo sauce
- 2 tbsp olive oil (for drizzling)

Instructions:

1. Preheat your oven to 400°F (200°C) and line a baking sheet with parchment paper.
2. In a bowl, mix together flour, water, garlic powder, onion powder, paprika, salt, and pepper.
3. Dip each cauliflower floret into the batter and place it on the baking sheet.
4. Drizzle with olive oil and bake for 20-25 minutes, or until crispy.
5. Once baked, toss the cauliflower in buffalo sauce.
6. Return to the oven for another 5-10 minutes to heat through.

7. Serve with ranch or blue cheese dressing. Enjoy!

Garlic Parmesan Roasted Potatoes

Ingredients:

- 1 lb baby potatoes (halved)
- 3 tbsp olive oil
- 3 garlic cloves (minced)
- 1/2 cup grated Parmesan cheese
- 1 tbsp dried rosemary
- Salt and pepper to taste
- Fresh parsley (for garnish)

Instructions:

1. Preheat your oven to 400°F (200°C).
2. In a bowl, toss the halved potatoes with olive oil, garlic, Parmesan, rosemary, salt, and pepper.
3. Spread the potatoes in a single layer on a baking sheet.
4. Roast for 25-30 minutes, or until the potatoes are golden and crispy.
5. Garnish with fresh parsley and serve immediately. Enjoy!

Cilantro Lime Rice

Ingredients:

- 1 cup long-grain white rice
- 2 cups water
- 1 tbsp olive oil
- 1/2 tsp salt
- 1/4 cup fresh cilantro (chopped)
- 1 lime (zested and juiced)

Instructions:

1. In a medium saucepan, bring water to a boil. Add rice, olive oil, and salt.
2. Reduce heat to low, cover, and simmer for 15-20 minutes, or until the rice is tender and water is absorbed.
3. Remove from heat and fluff the rice with a fork.
4. Stir in the cilantro, lime zest, and lime juice.
5. Serve as a side dish to tacos, grilled chicken, or any main dish. Enjoy!

Crispy Chickpeas

Ingredients:

- 1 can chickpeas (drained and rinsed)
- 1 tbsp olive oil
- 1 tsp smoked paprika
- 1/2 tsp garlic powder
- Salt and pepper to taste

Instructions:

1. Preheat your oven to 400°F (200°C) and line a baking sheet with parchment paper.
2. Pat the chickpeas dry with a paper towel and toss them in olive oil, smoked paprika, garlic powder, salt, and pepper.
3. Spread the chickpeas in a single layer on the baking sheet.
4. Roast for 25-30 minutes, shaking the pan halfway through, until crispy.
5. Serve as a snack or salad topping. Enjoy!

Tomato Basil Soup with Grilled Cheese

Ingredients for Soup:

- 2 tbsp olive oil
- 1 onion (diced)
- 2 garlic cloves (minced)
- 1 can (28 oz) crushed tomatoes
- 2 cups vegetable or chicken broth
- 1 tsp dried basil
- Salt and pepper to taste
- 1/4 cup heavy cream (optional)

Ingredients for Grilled Cheese:

- 4 slices bread
- 2 tbsp butter
- 4 slices cheese (cheddar, mozzarella, or your choice)

Instructions:

1. For the soup, heat olive oil in a large pot over medium heat. Add the onion and garlic, and cook until softened (5-7 minutes).

2. Add the crushed tomatoes, broth, basil, salt, and pepper. Bring to a simmer and cook for 15-20 minutes.

3. Use an immersion blender to puree the soup until smooth, or leave it chunky if you prefer.

4. Stir in heavy cream if desired, and adjust seasoning.

5. For the grilled cheese, butter each slice of bread and place cheese in between. Grill in a skillet over medium heat for 3-4 minutes per side, until golden and crispy.

6. Serve the soup with the grilled cheese on the side, and enjoy!

Coconut Curry Shrimp

Ingredients:

- 1 lb shrimp (peeled and deveined)
- 1 tbsp olive oil
- 1 onion (diced)
- 2 garlic cloves (minced)
- 1 tbsp grated ginger
- 1 tbsp curry powder
- 1 can (14 oz) coconut milk
- 1/2 cup chicken broth
- Salt and pepper to taste
- Fresh cilantro (for garnish)

Instructions:

1. Heat olive oil in a large skillet over medium heat. Add the onion, garlic, and ginger, and cook until softened (5 minutes).
2. Stir in curry powder and cook for 1 minute to bloom the spices.
3. Add the coconut milk and chicken broth, and bring to a simmer.
4. Add the shrimp and cook for 3-5 minutes, or until pink and cooked through.
5. Season with salt and pepper to taste.
6. Garnish with fresh cilantro and serve with rice or naan. Enjoy!

Balsamic Roasted Tomatoes

Ingredients:

- 2 cups cherry or grape tomatoes (halved)
- 2 tbsp balsamic vinegar
- 1 tbsp olive oil
- 1 tbsp fresh basil (chopped)
- Salt and pepper to taste

Instructions:

1. Preheat your oven to 400°F (200°C).
2. Toss the halved tomatoes with balsamic vinegar, olive oil, salt, and pepper.
3. Spread them in a single layer on a baking sheet.
4. Roast for 15-20 minutes, until the tomatoes are tender and caramelized.
5. Garnish with fresh basil and serve as a side dish or topping for pasta. Enjoy!

Lemon Garlic Hummus

Ingredients:

- 1 can (15 oz) chickpeas (drained and rinsed)
- 1/4 cup tahini
- 2 tbsp fresh lemon juice
- 2 garlic cloves
- 2 tbsp olive oil (plus more for drizzling)
- 2-3 tbsp water (as needed)
- Salt to taste
- Paprika and parsley for garnish (optional)

Instructions:

1. In a food processor, blend chickpeas, tahini, lemon juice, garlic, olive oil, and salt.
2. Add water gradually until you reach your desired consistency.
3. Taste and adjust lemon, salt, or garlic as desired.
4. Spoon into a bowl, drizzle with olive oil, and garnish with paprika and parsley if using. Enjoy with pita or veggies!

Sesame Crusted Tuna Bites

Ingredients:

- 8 oz ahi tuna (cut into bite-sized cubes)
- 2 tbsp soy sauce
- 1 tbsp sesame oil
- 1/2 tsp grated ginger
- 1/4 cup white sesame seeds
- 1/4 cup black sesame seeds
- Oil for searing

Instructions:

1. Toss tuna cubes with soy sauce, sesame oil, and ginger; marinate for 10 minutes.
2. Mix sesame seeds on a plate and coat each tuna cube thoroughly.
3. Heat a skillet with a little oil over high heat. Sear tuna for 30 seconds per side.
4. Serve immediately with soy sauce or spicy mayo. Enjoy!

Pineapple Teriyaki Chicken Skewers

Ingredients:

- 1 lb chicken breast (cubed)
- 1 cup fresh pineapple chunks
- 1/3 cup teriyaki sauce
- 1 tbsp honey
- 1 garlic clove (minced)
- 1 red bell pepper (cut into pieces)
- Skewers (soaked if wooden)

Instructions:

1. Whisk together teriyaki sauce, honey, and garlic. Marinate chicken in mixture for 30+ minutes.
2. Thread chicken, pineapple, and pepper onto skewers.
3. Grill or broil skewers for 12–15 minutes, turning and basting with marinade halfway.
4. Serve hot over rice or greens. Enjoy!

Crispy Fish Tacos with Lime Crema

Ingredients:

- 1 lb white fish (cod, tilapia, etc.)
- 1/2 cup flour
- 1/2 tsp paprika
- Salt & pepper
- Oil for frying
- Small tortillas
- Shredded cabbage or slaw mix

For Lime Crema:

- 1/2 cup sour cream or Greek yogurt
- Juice of 1 lime
- 1 tsp lime zest
- Salt to taste

Instructions:

1. Mix flour, paprika, salt, and pepper. Dredge fish pieces in mixture.
2. Fry fish in hot oil until golden and crispy; drain on paper towels.
3. Mix lime crema ingredients together.
4. Assemble tacos with cabbage, fish, and a drizzle of crema. Enjoy!

Spicy Roasted Sweet Potatoes

Ingredients:

- 2 large sweet potatoes (cubed)
- 2 tbsp olive oil
- 1 tsp chili powder
- 1/2 tsp smoked paprika
- 1/4 tsp cayenne pepper (optional)
- Salt and pepper to taste

Instructions:

1. Preheat oven to 425°F (220°C).
2. Toss sweet potatoes with oil and spices.
3. Spread on a baking sheet and roast 25–30 minutes, flipping halfway.
4. Serve as a side or in bowls and wraps. Enjoy!

Cheese Stuffed Peppers

Ingredients:

- 6 mini bell peppers (halved and deseeded)
- 1/2 cup cream cheese
- 1/4 cup shredded cheddar
- 1/4 cup mozzarella
- 1/2 tsp garlic powder
- Chopped chives or parsley for garnish

Instructions:

1. Preheat oven to 375°F (190°C).
2. Mix cheeses and garlic powder together.
3. Stuff each pepper half with the cheese mixture.
4. Bake for 15–20 minutes, until bubbly and golden.
5. Garnish and serve warm. Enjoy!

Avocado Mango Smoothie

Ingredients:

- 1 ripe avocado
- 1 cup fresh or frozen mango
- 1 banana
- 1 cup coconut milk (or any milk)
- 1 tbsp honey or maple syrup (optional)
- Ice cubes (optional)

Instructions:

1. Blend all ingredients in a high-speed blender until smooth.
2. Taste and adjust sweetness or consistency as needed.
3. Pour into a glass and enjoy chilled!

Roasted Red Pepper Soup

Ingredients:

- 4 red bell peppers (roasted and peeled, or 1 jar roasted red peppers)
- 1 tbsp olive oil
- 1 onion (chopped)
- 2 garlic cloves (minced)
- 1 1/2 cups vegetable broth
- 1/4 cup cream or coconut milk (optional)
- Salt and pepper to taste
- Fresh basil for garnish

Instructions:

1. Sauté onion and garlic in olive oil until soft.
2. Add roasted peppers and broth. Simmer for 10 minutes.
3. Blend until smooth and return to pot. Stir in cream if using.
4. Season and garnish with basil. Enjoy with bread or grilled cheese!

Garlic Herb Butter Steak

Ingredients:

- 2 ribeye or sirloin steaks (room temp)
- Salt and pepper to taste
- 2 tbsp olive oil
- 3 tbsp butter
- 3 garlic cloves (crushed)
- 1 tsp fresh rosemary (chopped)
- 1 tsp fresh thyme (chopped)

Instructions:

1. Season steaks generously with salt and pepper.
2. Heat olive oil in a skillet over high heat. Sear steaks 3–4 minutes per side.
3. Reduce heat, add butter, garlic, rosemary, and thyme. Spoon melted butter over steaks for 1–2 minutes.
4. Remove from heat and let rest for 5 minutes before slicing. Serve with drizzled herb butter.

Cucumber Feta Salad

Ingredients:

- 2 cucumbers (sliced)
- 1/2 red onion (thinly sliced)
- 1/2 cup crumbled feta cheese
- 1 tbsp olive oil
- 1 tbsp lemon juice
- Salt and pepper to taste
- Fresh dill or parsley for garnish

Instructions:

1. Combine cucumber, onion, and feta in a bowl.
2. Toss with olive oil, lemon juice, salt, and pepper.
3. Garnish with fresh herbs and chill before serving.

Baked Avocado Eggs

Ingredients:

- 2 ripe avocados (halved, pits removed)
- 4 small eggs
- Salt and pepper
- Chili flakes or fresh herbs (optional)

Instructions:

1. Preheat oven to 425°F (220°C).
2. Scoop a little avocado flesh to make space for the egg. Crack an egg into each half.
3. Bake for 12–15 minutes, until egg whites are set.
4. Season and garnish. Serve warm with toast.

Miso Soup with Tofu

Ingredients:

- 3 cups dashi broth or water
- 2 tbsp miso paste
- 1/2 cup soft tofu (cubed)
- 1 green onion (sliced)
- 1 tbsp wakame seaweed (rehydrated)

Instructions:

1. Heat broth until hot but not boiling.
2. In a small bowl, dissolve miso paste in a bit of hot broth, then stir into pot.
3. Add tofu and seaweed. Simmer 2–3 minutes.
4. Garnish with green onion and serve immediately.

Roasted Butternut Squash Soup

Ingredients:

- 1 medium butternut squash (peeled, cubed)
- 1 onion (chopped)
- 2 garlic cloves (peeled)
- 3 cups vegetable broth
- 2 tbsp olive oil
- 1/2 tsp ground nutmeg
- Salt and pepper to taste
- 1/2 cup cream or coconut milk (optional)

Instructions:

1. Toss squash, onion, and garlic with olive oil. Roast at 400°F (200°C) for 25–30 minutes.
2. Blend roasted veggies with broth until smooth.
3. Pour into a pot, add nutmeg, and simmer. Stir in cream if desired.
4. Season and serve warm with crusty bread.

Crispy Garlic Parmesan Brussel Sprouts

Ingredients:

- 1 lb Brussels sprouts (halved)
- 3 tbsp olive oil
- 3 garlic cloves (minced)
- 1/4 cup grated Parmesan cheese
- Salt and pepper to taste

Instructions:

1. Preheat oven to 425°F (220°C).
2. Toss sprouts with olive oil, garlic, salt, and pepper.
3. Spread on a baking sheet, cut-side down. Roast for 20–25 minutes.
4. Sprinkle with Parmesan and roast 5 more minutes. Serve crispy and hot!

Tomato Cucumber Salad with Feta

Ingredients:

- 2 cups cherry tomatoes (halved)
- 1 cucumber (sliced)
- 1/4 red onion (sliced thin)
- 1/2 cup feta cheese (crumbled)
- 2 tbsp olive oil
- 1 tbsp red wine vinegar
- Salt and pepper
- Fresh oregano or parsley

Instructions:

1. Combine tomatoes, cucumber, onion, and feta in a bowl.
2. Whisk olive oil, vinegar, salt, and pepper. Pour over salad and toss.
3. Garnish with herbs. Chill before serving.

Honey Mustard Chicken Bites

Ingredients:

- 1 lb chicken breast (cut into bite-size pieces)
- 2 tbsp olive oil
- Salt and pepper to taste

For Honey Mustard Sauce:

- 2 tbsp Dijon mustard
- 2 tbsp honey
- 1 tbsp mayonnaise (optional for creaminess)
- 1 tsp apple cider vinegar

Instructions:

1. Season chicken and sauté in olive oil until golden and cooked through.
2. Whisk sauce ingredients together.
3. Toss chicken in sauce or serve as dip on the side.

Black Bean and Corn Salsa

Ingredients:

- 1 can black beans (drained and rinsed)
- 1 cup corn kernels (fresh, canned, or thawed from frozen)
- 1/2 red onion (finely chopped)
- 1 tomato (diced)
- 1/4 cup chopped cilantro
- Juice of 1 lime
- Salt and pepper to taste
- Optional: 1 jalapeño (seeded and minced)

Instructions:

1. Combine all ingredients in a large bowl.
2. Toss well and let sit for 10–15 minutes before serving.
3. Serve with tortilla chips or as a taco topping.

Spinach and Feta Stuffed Chicken

Ingredients:

- 2 large chicken breasts
- 1 cup fresh spinach (chopped)
- 1/2 cup feta cheese (crumbled)
- 1 clove garlic (minced)
- Salt and pepper
- 1 tbsp olive oil

Instructions:

1. Preheat oven to 375°F (190°C).
2. Slice a pocket into each chicken breast.
3. In a bowl, mix spinach, feta, garlic, salt, and pepper.
4. Stuff the mixture into chicken breasts and secure with toothpicks.
5. Sear in a skillet with olive oil until golden, then transfer to oven and bake for 20–25 minutes.

Lemon Parmesan Asparagus

Ingredients:

- 1 bunch asparagus (trimmed)
- 2 tbsp olive oil
- 2 tbsp lemon juice
- 1/4 cup grated Parmesan
- Salt and pepper

Instructions:

1. Preheat oven to 400°F (200°C).
2. Toss asparagus with olive oil, lemon juice, salt, and pepper.
3. Place on a baking sheet and sprinkle with Parmesan.
4. Roast for 12–15 minutes until tender and golden.

Spicy Tuna Tartare

Ingredients:

- 6 oz sushi-grade tuna (finely diced)
- 1 tbsp soy sauce
- 1 tsp sesame oil
- 1/2 tsp sriracha or chili paste
- 1 tsp lime juice
- 1 green onion (sliced)
- 1/2 avocado (optional, diced)

Instructions:

1. Mix all ingredients gently in a bowl.
2. Taste and adjust spice or seasoning as needed.
3. Serve chilled with crackers, cucumber rounds, or wonton chips.

Smoked Salmon Crostini

Ingredients:

- 1 baguette (sliced)
- 4 oz cream cheese (softened)
- 4 oz smoked salmon
- 1 tbsp capers
- Fresh dill
- Lemon zest

Instructions:

1. Toast baguette slices until golden.
2. Spread with cream cheese.
3. Top with smoked salmon, a few capers, dill, and a sprinkle of lemon zest.
4. Serve immediately.

Creamy Garlic Parmesan Mushrooms

Ingredients:

- 1 tbsp butter
- 1 tbsp olive oil
- 2 cups mushrooms (halved or sliced)
- 2 garlic cloves (minced)
- 1/3 cup heavy cream
- 1/4 cup grated Parmesan
- Salt and pepper to taste
- Parsley for garnish

Instructions:

1. Heat butter and oil in a pan. Sauté mushrooms until browned.
2. Add garlic and cook for 1 minute.
3. Stir in cream and Parmesan. Simmer for 3–5 minutes until thick.
4. Season and garnish with parsley.

Roasted Carrot Hummus

Ingredients:

- 2 carrots (peeled and chopped)
- 1 can chickpeas (drained)
- 2 tbsp tahini
- 2 tbsp lemon juice
- 1 garlic clove
- 2 tbsp olive oil
- Salt and cumin to taste

Instructions:

1. Roast carrots at 400°F (200°C) for 25 minutes.
2. In a blender, combine all ingredients and blend until smooth.
3. Add water or more olive oil to adjust consistency.
4. Serve with pita or veggies.

Bacon Wrapped Dates

Ingredients:

- 12 pitted Medjool dates
- 6 slices of bacon (cut in half)
- Optional: 12 almonds or small cubes of cheese (stuffing)

Instructions:

1. Preheat oven to 400°F (200°C).
2. (Optional) Stuff each date with an almond or cheese cube.
3. Wrap each date with half a slice of bacon and secure with a toothpick.
4. Bake for 15–20 minutes, turning halfway, until bacon is crisp.
5. Let cool slightly before serving.

Buffalo Cauliflower Salad

Ingredients:

- 1 small head cauliflower (cut into florets)
- 1/4 cup buffalo sauce
- 1 tbsp olive oil
- 4 cups mixed greens
- 1/2 cup cherry tomatoes (halved)
- 1/4 cup shredded carrots
- 1/4 cup blue cheese or ranch dressing (optional)
- Green onions for garnish

Instructions:

1. Preheat oven to 425°F (220°C).
2. Toss cauliflower with olive oil and buffalo sauce. Roast for 25 minutes until crispy.
3. In a large bowl, combine greens, tomatoes, carrots, and warm cauliflower.
4. Drizzle with dressing and garnish with green onions.

Apple Cinnamon Baked Oatmeal

Ingredients:

- 2 cups rolled oats
- 1 tsp cinnamon
- 1/2 tsp nutmeg
- 1/2 tsp baking powder
- 1/4 tsp salt
- 2 cups milk (or dairy-free)
- 1/4 cup maple syrup or honey
- 1 egg
- 1 apple (diced)
- 1 tsp vanilla extract
- Optional: nuts or raisins

Instructions:

1. Preheat oven to 375°F (190°C). Grease a baking dish.
2. In a bowl, mix oats, spices, baking powder, and salt.
3. In another bowl, whisk milk, maple syrup, egg, and vanilla. Combine with dry mix.
4. Fold in apples (and optional add-ins). Pour into dish.
5. Bake for 35–40 minutes. Let cool slightly before serving.

Pumpkin Spice Granola

Ingredients:

- 3 cups rolled oats
- 1/2 cup pumpkin puree
- 1/3 cup maple syrup or honey
- 1/4 cup coconut oil (melted)
- 1 tsp cinnamon
- 1/2 tsp nutmeg
- 1/4 tsp cloves
- 1/2 tsp salt
- Optional: nuts, seeds, dried cranberries

Instructions:

1. Preheat oven to 325°F (160°C).
2. In a large bowl, mix oats, spices, salt, and optional nuts/seeds.
3. In another bowl, whisk pumpkin, syrup, and oil. Pour over oats and mix well.
4. Spread onto a lined baking sheet and bake for 30–35 minutes, stirring halfway.
5. Let cool completely before storing. Add dried fruit if desired.

Crispy Fried Green Beans

Ingredients:

- 1/2 lb green beans (trimmed)
- 1/2 cup flour
- 2 eggs (beaten)
- 1 cup panko breadcrumbs
- Salt and pepper
- Oil for frying
- Optional: dipping sauce (ranch, aioli, etc.)

Instructions:

1. Heat oil in a pan to 350°F (175°C).
2. Dredge beans in flour, dip in egg, then coat in breadcrumbs.
3. Fry in batches until golden (2–3 mins). Drain on paper towels.
4. Season and serve hot with your favorite dip.

Lemon Basil Pesto Pasta

Ingredients:

- 8 oz pasta of choice
- 2 cups fresh basil leaves
- 1/3 cup grated Parmesan
- 1/3 cup olive oil
- 1 garlic clove
- Zest and juice of 1 lemon
- Salt and pepper to taste
- Optional: cherry tomatoes or pine nuts

Instructions:

1. Cook pasta until al dente. Reserve 1/4 cup pasta water.
2. In a food processor, blend basil, Parmesan, garlic, lemon zest/juice, and olive oil.
3. Toss pesto with drained pasta, adding pasta water as needed for creaminess.
4. Season and top with cherry tomatoes or pine nuts if desired.

www.ingramcontent.com/pod-product-compliance
Lightning Source LLC
LaVergne TN
LVHW081322060526
838201LV00055B/2415